★ COUNTRY HITS ★
for Ukulele

ISBN 978-1-4803-9613-5

HAL•LEONARD®
CORPORATION
7777 W. BLUEMOUND RD. P.O. BOX 13819 MILWAUKEE, WI 53213

For all works contained herein:
Unauthorized copying, arranging, adapting, recording, Internet posting, public performance,
or other distribution of the printed music in this publication is an infringement of copyright.
Infringers are liable under the law.

Visit Hal Leonard Online at
www.halleonard.com

★ CONTENTS ★

Ain't Nothing 'Bout You

Words and Music by Tom Shapiro and Rivers Rutherford

1. Once I thought that love was some-thin' I could nev-er do. ___
2. In my life I've been ___ ham-mered by some heav-y blows ___

Nev-er knew that I could feel this much.
that ___ nev-er knocked me off my feet.

But this yearn-in' in the deep part of my heart for you ___
All you got-ta do is smile at me, and down I go. ___

is more than a re-ac-tion to your
And, ba-by, it's no mys-ter-

Copyright © 2000 Sony/ATV Music Publishing LLC, Wenonga Music and Universal Music Corp.
All Rights on behalf of Sony/ATV Music Publishing LLC and Wenonga Music Administered by
Sony/ATV Music Publishing LLC, 424 Church Street, Suite 1200, Nashville, TN 37219
International Copyright Secured   All Rights Reserved

touch. It's a per - fect pas - sion and I can't
y why I sur - ren - der. Girl, you've got

Chorus

get e - nough. ⎫
ev -'ry - thing. ⎭ The way you look, the way you laugh, the way you love with all you have, there ain't

noth - in' 'bout __ you that don't do some - thin' for __ me. The way you

kiss, the way you cry, the way you move when you walk by, there ain't

noth - in' 'bout __ you that don't do some - thin' for __ me.

1.

Whoa. _____

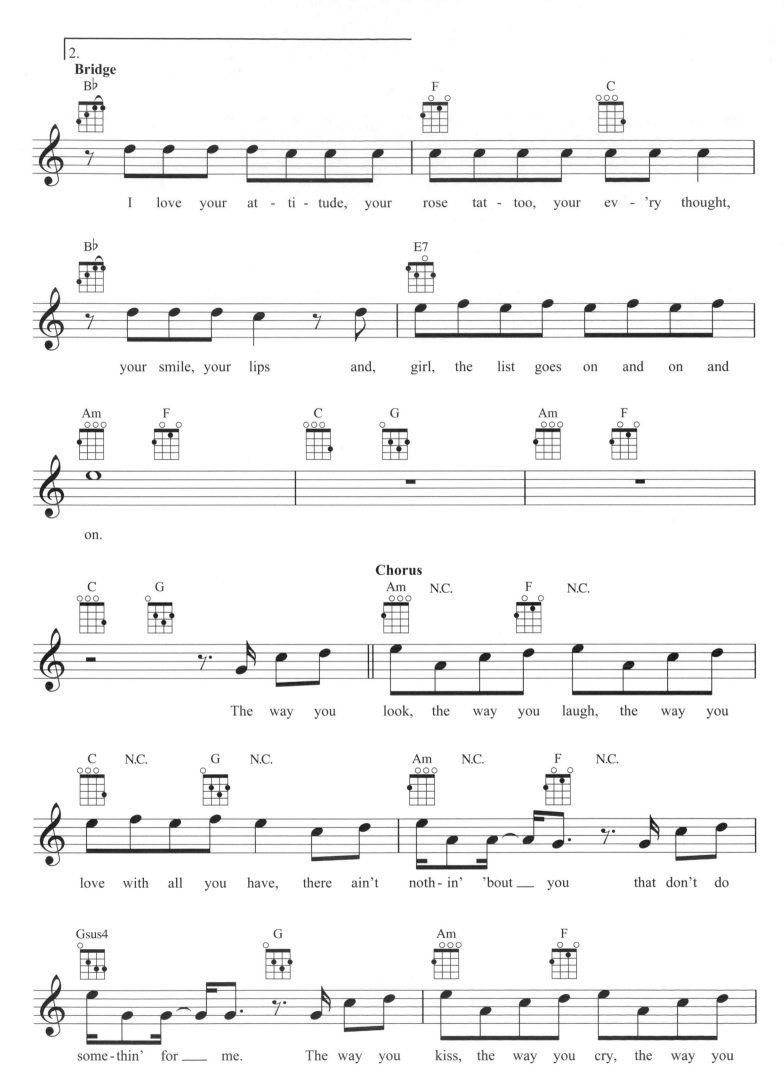

2.

Bridge

B♭　　　　　　　　　　　　　　　　F　　　　　　　　　C

I love your at - ti - tude, your rose tat - too, your ev - 'ry thought,

B♭　　　　　　　　　　　　　　　E7

your smile, your lips and, girl, the list goes on and on and

Am　　F　　　　C　　G　　　Am　　F

on.

Chorus

C　　G　　　　Am　　N.C.　　F　　N.C.

The way you look, the way you laugh, the way you

C　N.C.　G　N.C.　　Am　N.C.　　F　N.C.

love with all you have, there ain't noth - in' 'bout ___ you that don't do

Gsus4　　　　　　G　　　Am　　F

some - thin' for ___ me. The way you kiss, the way you cry, the way you

As Good As I Once Was

Words and Music by Toby Keith and Scotty Emerick

First note

Moderately
N.C.

Verse

1. She said, "I've seen you in here _____ be - fore."
(2.) _____ friend, Dave.

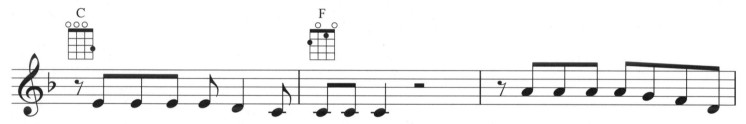

I said, "I've been here a time or two."   She said, "Hel - lo, my name is
I've known him since we were kids at school.   Last night he had a few shots,

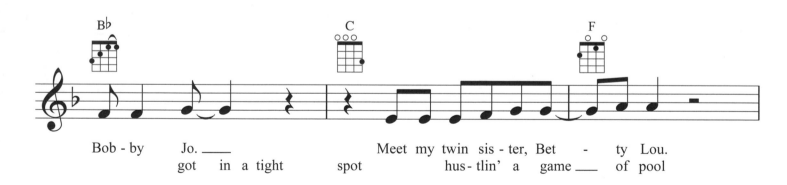

Bob - by Jo. _____   Meet my twin sis - ter, Bet - ty Lou.
got in a tight spot   hus - tlin' a game ___ of pool

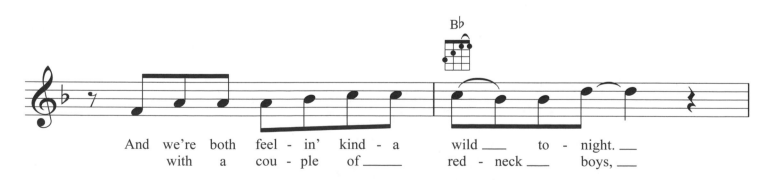

And we're both feel - in' kind - a wild ___ to - night. ___
with a cou - ple of ___ red - neck ___ boys, ___

Copyright © 2004 Tokeco Tunes, Sony/ATV Music Publishing LLC, Big Yellow Dog Music and Florida Cracker Music
All Rights on behalf of Sony/ATV Music Publishing LLC, Big Yellow Dog Music and Florida Cracker Music Administered by
Sony/ATV Music Publishing LLC, 424 Church Street, Suite 1200, Nashville, TN 37219
All Rights Reserved   Used by Permission

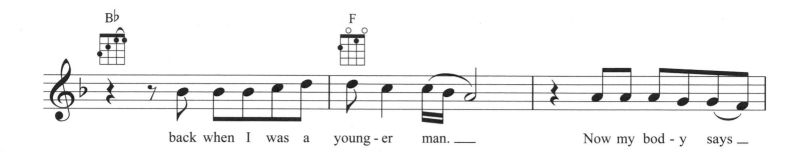

back when I was a young-er man. ___ Now my bod-y says ___

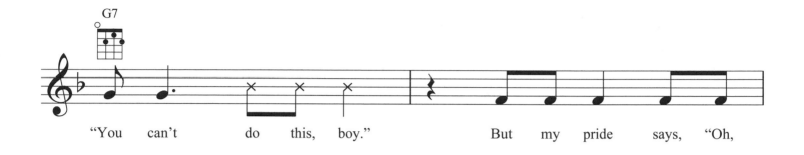

"You can't do this, boy." But my pride says, "Oh,

D.S. al Coda

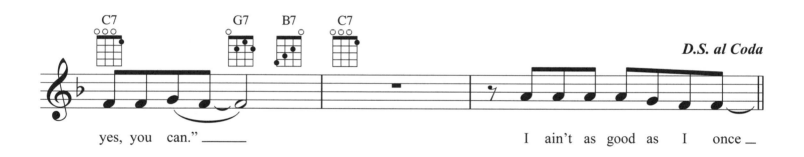

yes, you can." ___ I ain't as good as I once ___

Coda

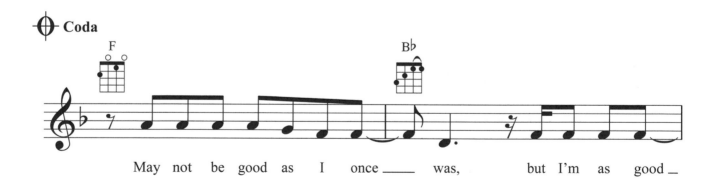

May not be good as I once ___ was, but I'm as good ___

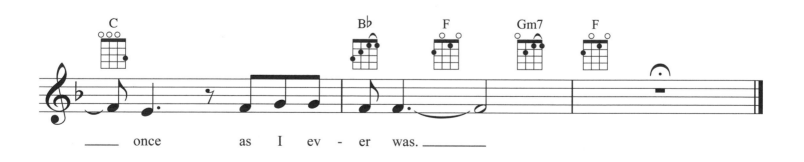

___ once as I ev - er was. ___

Beautiful Mess

Words and Music by Sonny LeMaire, Clay Mills and Shane Minor

1. Go - in' out of my mind these days, _____
like I'm walk - in' 'round in a haze. ____ ____
I can't ____ think straight,
I can't con - cen - trate ____ and I need a shave.

2. I go to work and I ____ look tired. ____
3. This morn - in' put ____ salt in my cof - fee. ____

© 2002 RESERVOIR MEDIA MANAGEMENT, INC., MONKEY C MUSIC, API COUNTRY MUSIC,
BMG MONARCH, CREATIVE ARTISTS AGENCY PUBLISHING, EMI BLACKWOOD MUSIC INC. and SHANE MINOR MUSIC
All Rights for RESERVOIR MEDIA MANAGEMENT, INC., MONKEY C MUSIC
and API COUNTRY MUSIC Controlled and Administered by AFFILIATED PUBLISHERS, INC.
All Rights for BMG MONARCH and CREATIVE ARTISTS AGENCY PUBLISHING Administered by BMG RIGHTS MANAGEMENT (US) LLC
All Rights for SHANE MINOR MUSIC Controlled and Administered by EMI BLACKWOOD MUSIC INC.
All Rights Reserved   International Copyright Secured   Used by Permission

Am

The boss man says, "Son, you're gon-na get
I put my shoes on the wrong _____

C   Dm

fired. _____   This ain't your _ style."
feet. _____   I'm los-in' my mind, _ I ___ swear.

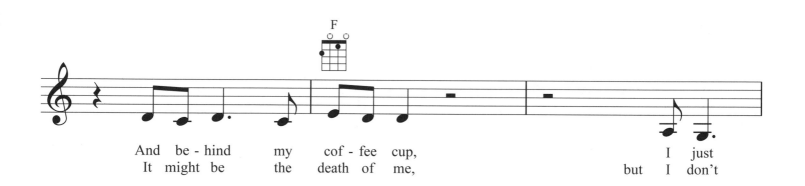

F

And be-hind my cof-fee cup,   I just
It might be the death of me,   but I don't

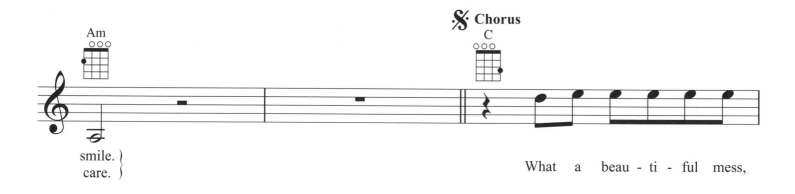

Am   𝄋 Chorus
                                C

smile. ⎫
care. ⎭   What a beau-ti-ful mess,

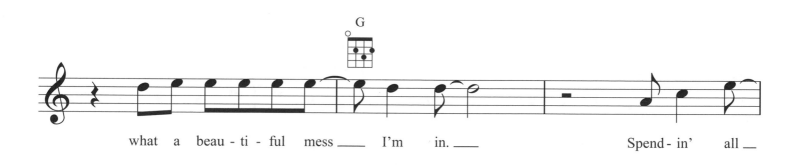

G

what a beau-ti-ful mess ___ I'm in. ___   Spend-in' all __

_____ my time _____ with you, _____ there's noth - in' else _____ I'd rath -

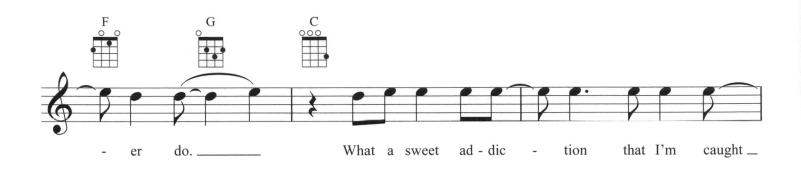

- er do. _____ What a sweet ad - dic - tion that I'm caught _____

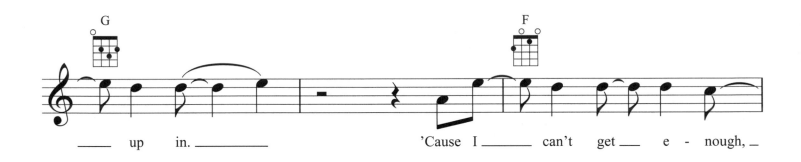

_____ up in. _____ 'Cause I _____ can't get _____ e - nough, _____

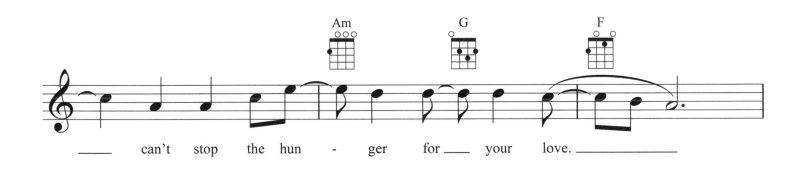

_____ can't stop the hun - ger for _____ your love. _____

To Coda ⊕ | 1.

What a beau - ti - ful, what a beau - ti - ful mess _____ I'm in, _____

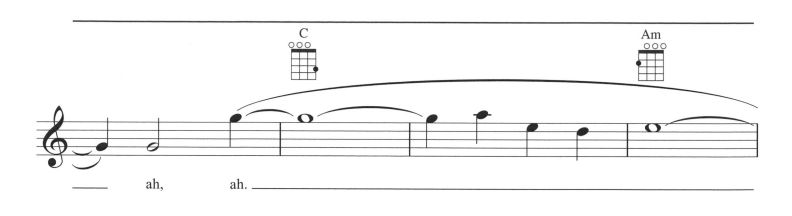

ah, ah.

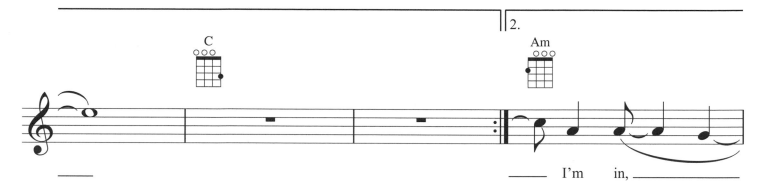

I'm in,

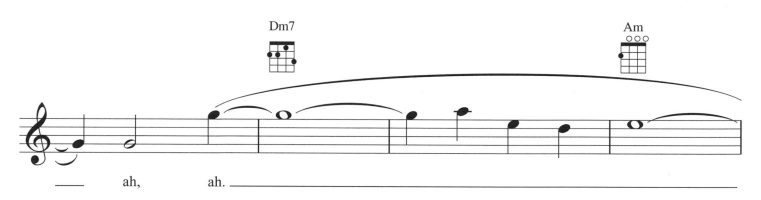

ah, ah.

Bridge

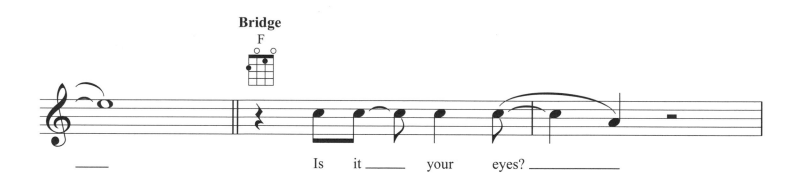

Is it ___ your eyes? ___

Is it ___ your smile? ___ All I

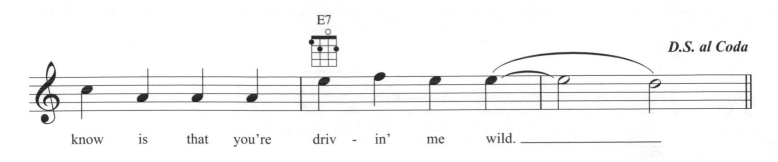

D.S. al Coda

know   is   that   you're   driv - in'   me   wild. _____

Coda

____ I'm   in, _____   ah,   ah. _____

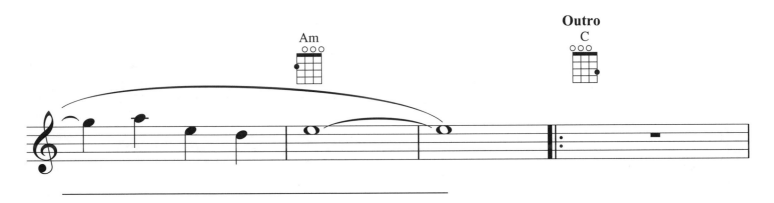

Outro

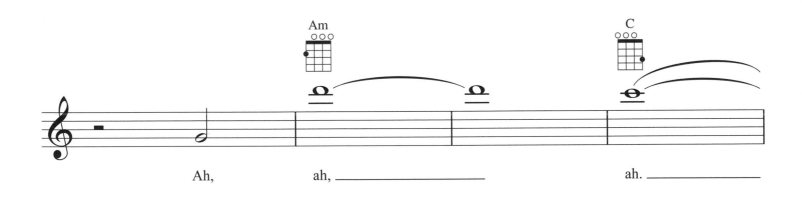

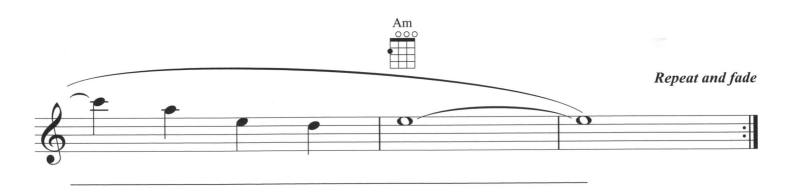

Ah,   ah, _____   ah. _____

Repeat and fade

Blessed

Words and Music by Brett James, Hillary Lindsey and Troy Verges

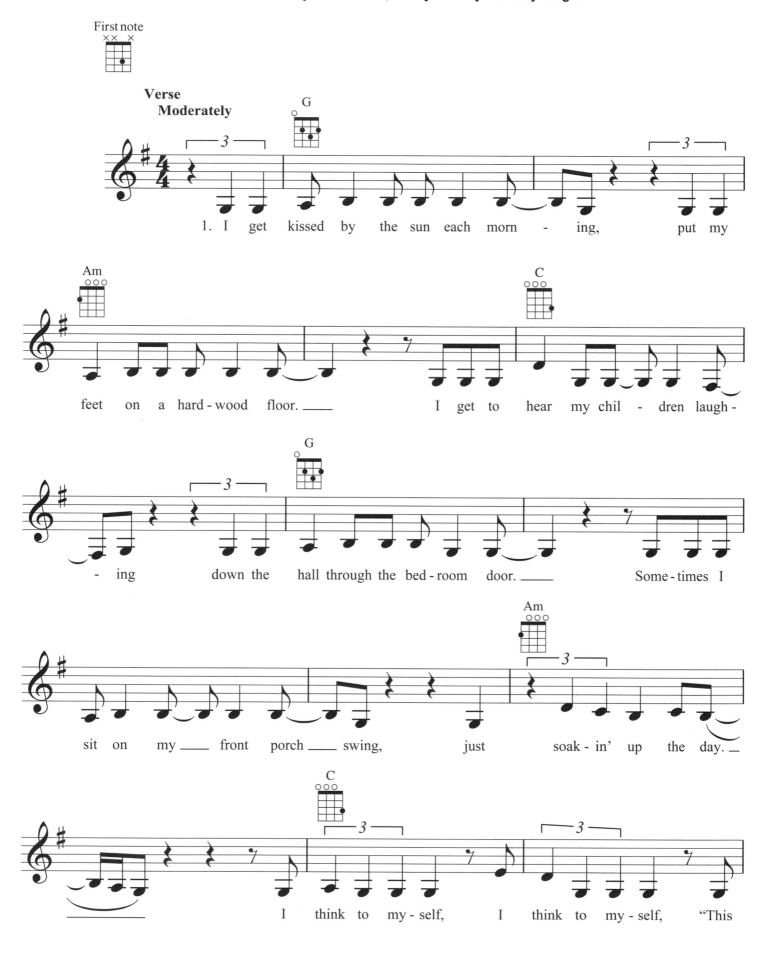

Copyright © 2001 Sony/ATV Music Publishing LLC, Onaly Music, Animal Fair and Songs Of Universal, Inc.
All Rights on behalf of Sony/ATV Music Publishing LLC, Onaly Music and Animal Fair Administered by
Sony/ATV Music Publishing LLC, 424 Church Street, Suite 1200, Nashville, TN 37219
International Copyright Secured   All Rights Reserved

Bridge

When I, when I'm sing - in' my kids to sleep, _____

when I feel you hold - in' me, _____ I _____

Chorus

know _____ I am so blessed. _ And I feel like I

found _ my way. _____ I thank God _ for all _____ I've been

giv - en at the end of ev - er - y day. _____ I have been

blessed _____ with so much more than I _____ de - serve, _

to be   here   with   the   ones   who   love   me,   to   love

them   so   much   it   hurts.   I   have   been   blessed.   Oh,   yes,

I   have   been   blessed,   oh,   yeah,   yeah.

Outro

I   have   been   blessed,

I   have   been   blessed.

Repeat and fade

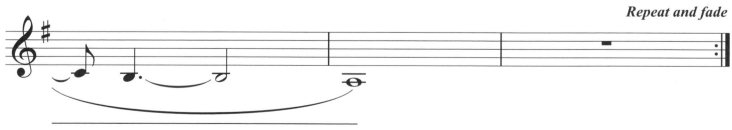

21

Before He Cheats

Words and Music by Josh Kear and Chris Tompkins

Copyright © 2005 Sony/ATV Music Publishing LLC, Mighty Underdog Music and Big Loud Songs
All Rights on behalf of Sony/ATV Music Publishing LLC and Mighty Underdog Music Administered by
Sony/ATV Music Publishing LLC, 424 Church Street, Suite 1200, Nashville, TN 37219
All Rights on behalf of Big Loud Songs Administered by Big Loud Bucks
International Copyright Secured   All Rights Reserved

And he don't know _____
Oh, and he don't know _____

%: Chorus

_____ that I dug my key in-to the side _____ of his

pret-ty lit-tle souped-up four-wheel _____ drive, _____ carved my name in-

to his leath-er seat. _____ I took a

Lou-is-ville Slug-ger to both _____ head-lights, _____ slashed a hole _____ in all _____

To Coda ⊕

_____ four tires, _____ and may-be next time _____ he'll think _____ be-fore _____ he _____

Come a Little Closer

Words and Music by Dierks Bentley and Brett Beavers

Copyright © 2005 Sony/ATV Music Publishing LLC
All Rights Administered by Sony/ATV Music Publishing LLC, 424 Church Street, Suite 1200, Nashville, TN 37219
International Copyright Secured   All Rights Reserved

Girl, it's right __ here at our fin - ger - tips. __
and let it wash _____ all the hurt a - way. __
I wan - na be strong - er than we've ev - er been. __

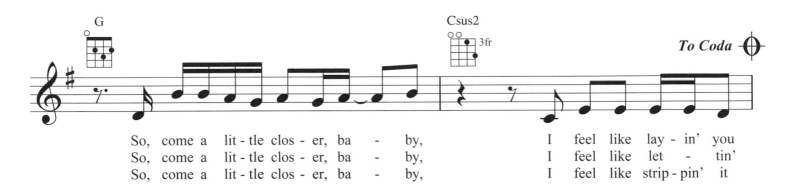

So, come a lit - tle clos - er, ba - by, I feel like lay - in' you
So, come a lit - tle clos - er, ba - by, I feel like let - tin'
So, come a lit - tle clos - er, ba - by, I feel like strip - pin' it

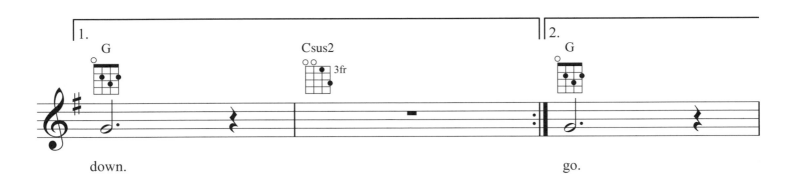

down. go.

Bridge

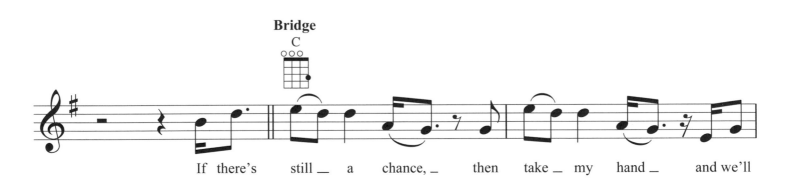

If there's still __ a chance, __ then take __ my hand __ and we'll

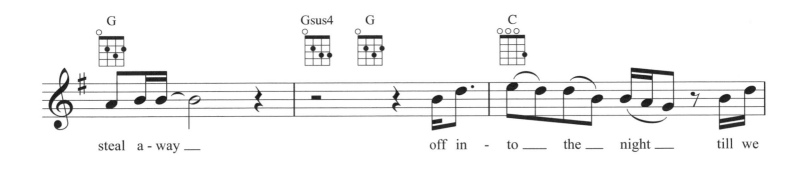

steal a - way __ off in - to ___ the __ night ___ till we

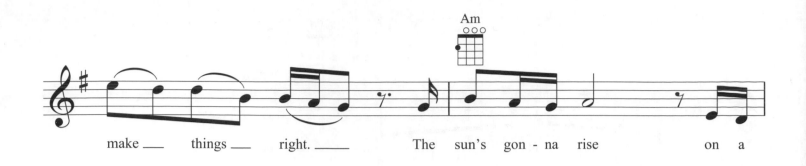

make ___ things ___ right. ___ The sun's gon-na rise on a

bet-ter day. ___ down.

Outro

Come a lit-tle clos-er, ba - by,

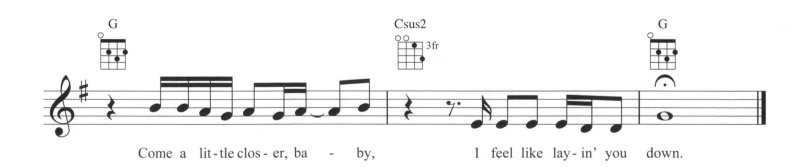

just a lit-tle bit clos-er, ba - by.

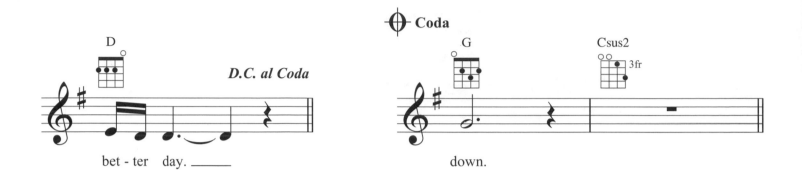

Come a lit-tle clos-er, ba - by, I feel like lay-in' you down.

Crash My Party

Words and Music by Ashley Gorley and Rodney Clawson

© 2013 SONGS OF SOUTHSIDE INDEPENDENT MUSIC PUBLISHING, EXTERNAL COMBUSTION MUSIC, OUT OF THE TAPEROOM MUSIC,
BIG RED TOE MUSIC and AMARILLO SKY SONGS
All Rights for SONGS OF SOUTHSIDE INDEPENDENT MUSIC PUBLISHING, EXTERNAL COMBUSTION MUSIC
and OUT OF THE TAPEROOM MUSIC Administered by SONGS OF SOUTHSIDE INDEPENDENT PUBLISHING
All Rights for BIG RED TOE MUSIC and AMARILLO SKY SONGS Administered by BIG LOUD BUCKS
All Rights Reserved   Used by Permission

Pre-Chorus

Girl, _____ I don't care, _ oh, I just _____ got-ta see _ what you're wear-

- in'. Your hair, _____ is it pulled _ up or fall - in' _____ down? _

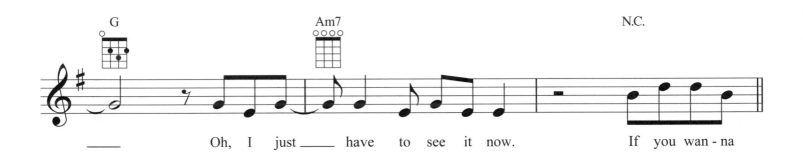

_____ Oh, I just _____ have to see it now. If you wan - na

Chorus

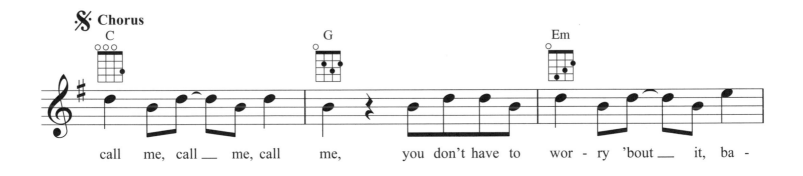

call me, call _ me, call me, you don't have to wor - ry 'bout _ it, ba -

by. You can wake me _ up _____ in the dead of the night. _ Wreck _ my plans, _

_____ ba - by, that's al - right. _____ And this is a drop _____ ev - 'ry - thing _

_____ kind - a thing. _ Swing on _ by, _ I'll _ pour _ you a drink. _ The door's _

_____ un - locked. _ I'll _ leave _ on the lights. _ Ba - by, you can crash _ my par -

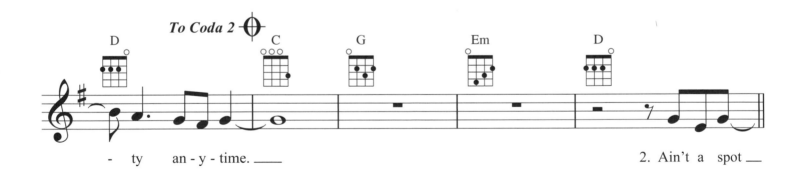

- ty an - y - time. _____ 2. Ain't a spot _

Verse

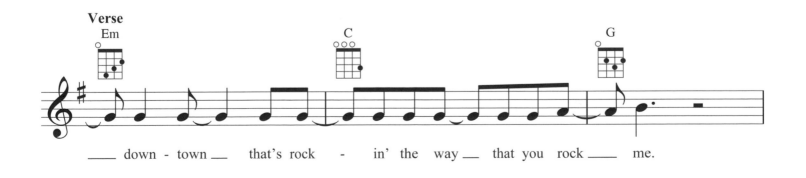

_____ down - town _ that's rock - in' the way _ that you rock _____ me.

Ain't a bar ___ that can make ___ me buzz ___ the way ___ that you do. ___

___ I could be on the front ___ row ___ of the best ___

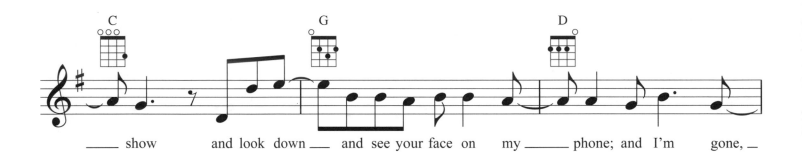

___ show and look down ___ and see your face on my ___ phone; and I'm gone, ___

___ so ___ long, hang ___ on. I'll meet ___ you in a min-ute or two. ___

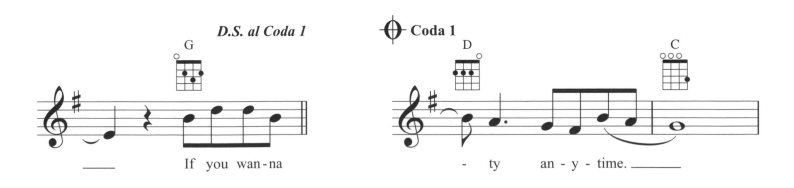

D.S. al Coda 1   ⊕ Coda 1

___ If you wan-na   - ty an-y-time. _____

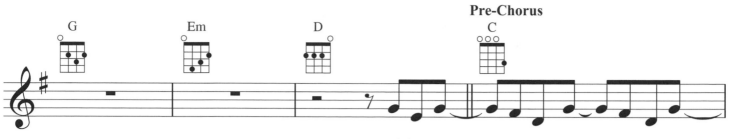

If it's two _____ in the morn - in' and you're _

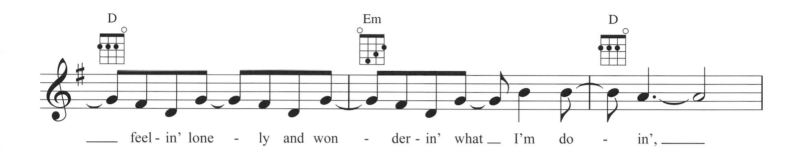

_____ feel - in' lone - ly and won - der - in' what _ I'm do - in', _____

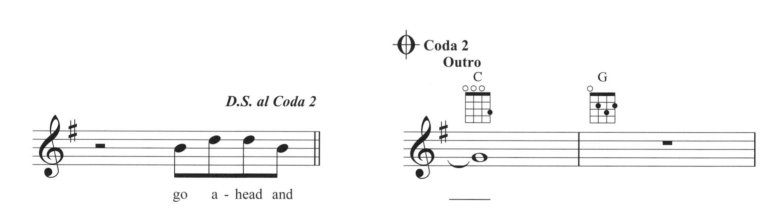

D.S. al Coda 2

go a - head and

Coda 2
Outro

_____

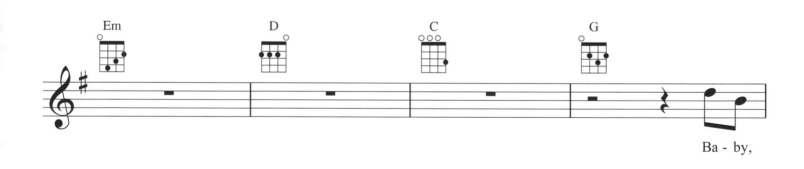

Ba - by,

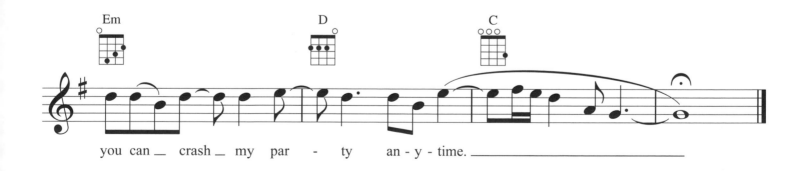

you can _ crash _ my par - ty an - y - time. _____

Cruise

Words and Music by Chase Rice, Tyler Hubbard, Brian Kelley, Joey Moi and Jesse Rice

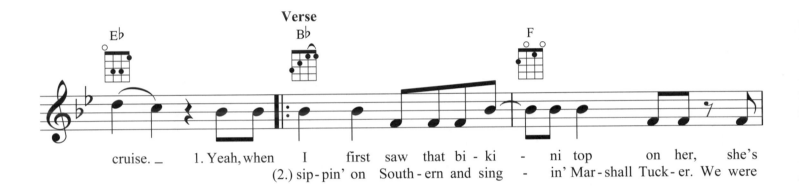

Copyright © 2012 Sony/ATV Music Publishing LLC, Dack Janiels Publishing, Big Loud Mountain,
Big Red Toe, Deep Fried Dreams and Artist Revolution Publishing
All Rights on behalf of Sony/ATV Music Publishing LLC and Dack Janiels Publishing Administered by
Sony/ATV Music Publishing LLC, 424 Church Street, Suite 1200, Nashville, TN 37219
All Rights on behalf of Big Loud Mountain, Big Red Toe and Deep Fried Dreams Administered by Big Loud Bucks
International Copyright Secured   All Rights Reserved

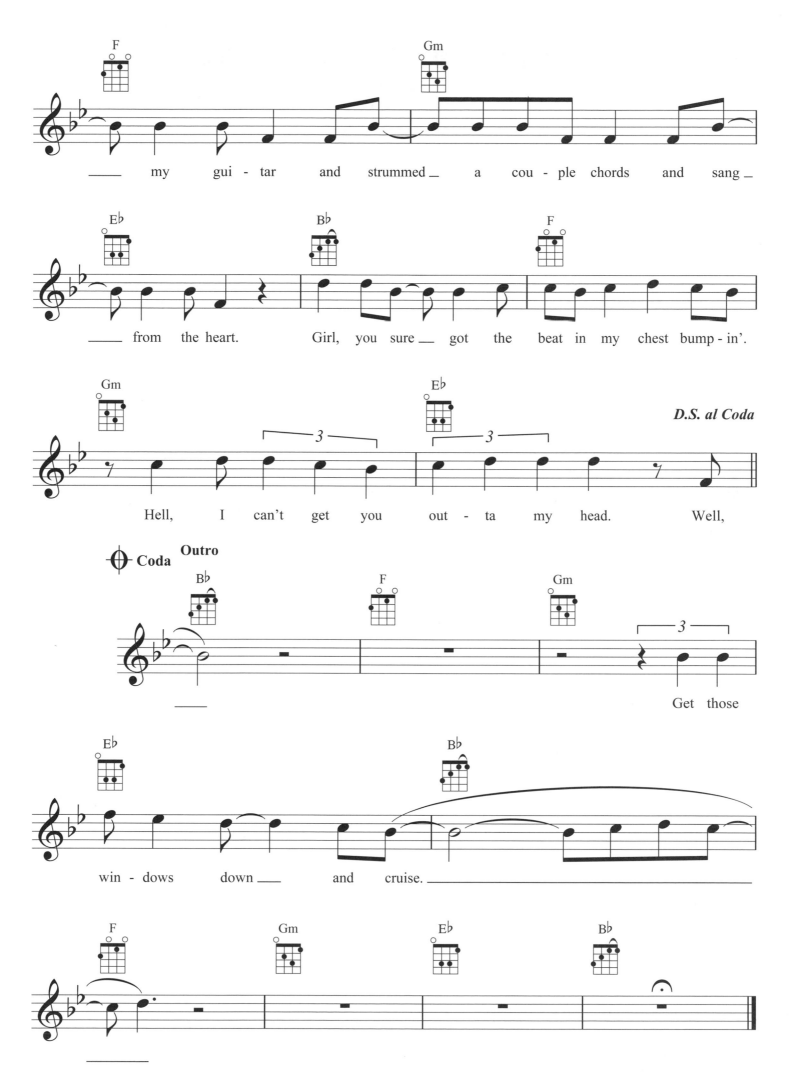

Don't You Wanna Stay

Words and Music by Jason Sellers, Paul Jenkins and Andrew Gibson

Copyright © 2010 Sony/ATV Music Publishing LLC, Becky's Boy Music and Godfather Rich Muzik
All Rights on behalf of Sony/ATV Music Publishing LLC and Becky's Boy Music Administered by Sony/ATV Music Publishing LLC,
424 Church Street, Suite 1200, Nashville, TN 37219
All Rights on behalf of Godfather Rich Muzik Administered by Kobalt Songs Music Publishing
International Copyright Secured   All Rights Reserved

Chorus

Both: Don't you wan - na stay here a lit - tle while? Don't you wan - na hold each oth - er tight? Don't you wan - na fall a - sleep with me to - night? Don't you wan - na stay here a lit - tle while? We can make for - ev - er feel this

To Coda

1.

way. Don't you wan - na stay?

Don't you wan - na stay? _____

Male: Oh, it feels ___ so per - fect,

Female:
ba - by. Yeah, it feels ___ so per - fect, ba - by. _____

_____ *Both:* Don't you wan - na stay here a

D.S. al Coda

lit - tle while? ___

Coda

Don't you wan - na stay? _____

_____ Yeah.

Female: Don't you wan - na stay? _____

Both: Yeah. _____

Yeah. _____

The Good Stuff

Words and Music by Craig Wiseman and Jim Collins

Copyright © 2002 by Universal Music - MGB Songs, Mrs. Lumpkin's Poodle, Warner-Tamerlane Publishing Corp. and Make Shift Music
All Rights for Mrs. Lumpkin's Poodle Administered by Big Loud Bucks
All Rights for Make Shift Music Administered by Warner-Tamerlane Publishing Corp.
International Copyright Secured   All Rights Reserved

good stuff." He did - n't reach a - round for the

whis - key, he did - n't pour me a beer. His

blue eyes kind - a went mist - y, he said, "You can't find __ that here. __

Chorus

__ 'Cause it's the first long kiss on a sec - ond date,

ma - ma's all wor - ried when you get home late __ and drop - pin' the ring __ in the spa -

ghet - ti plate 'cause your hands are shak - in' so much. And it's the

way that she looks _ with the rice ___ in her hair ___ and eat-in' burnt sup-pers the whole _

___ first year ___ and ask - in' for sec - onds to keep her from tear - in'

up. Yeah, man, that's the good stuff." _____

2. He grabbed a

Verse

car-ton of milk _ and he poured _ a glass. And I smiled _ and said, "I'll

have some of that." _ We sat there and talked _ as an hour passed like old _

44

Chorus

sight of her hold-in' my ba-by girl, the way she a-dored __ that string __ __ of pearls I gave __ her the day __ that our young - est boy Earl mar-ried his high - school love. __ And it's a new T - shirt __ say-in' I'm __ __ a grand-pa, be - in' right there __ as our time __ got small __ and hold - - in' her hand __ when the good Lord called _____ her up. __ Yeah, man, that's the good stuff." _____

Bridge

He said, "When you get home, __ she'll start __ __ to cry. When she says, 'I'm sor - ry,' say, 'So am I.' And look in - to __ those eyes __ so __ deep in love __ and drink it up __ 'cause that's the good stuff, __ that's the good stuff." __

I Hope You Dance

Words and Music by Tia Sillers and Mark D. Sanders

Verse
Moderately, in 2

1. I hope you nev - er lose _____ your sense of
(2.) nev - er fear _____ those _____ moun - tains in the

won - der.   You get your fill _____ to eat, _____ but al -
dis - tance.   Nev - er set - tle for _____ the path _____

- ways   keep   that   hun - ger.   May   you
_____ of   least   re - sist - ance.   Liv - in'

nev - er   take _____ one   sin - gle   breath _____ for grant - ed.
might mean   tak - in'   chanc - es   if they're worth tak - in'.

Copyright © 2000 Sony/ATV Music Publishing LLC, Choice Is Tragic Music, Universal Music Corp. and Soda Creek Songs
All Rights on behalf of Sony/ATV Music Publishing LLC and Choice Is Tragic Music Administered by
Sony/ATV Music Publishing LLC, 424 Church Street, Suite 1200, Nashville, TN 37219
All Rights on behalf of Soda Creek Songs Controlled and Administered by Universal Music Corp.
International Copyright Secured   All Rights Reserved

God for - bid _____ love ev - er leave _____ you emp - ty - hand -
Lov - in' might _____ be a mis - take, _____ but it's _____ worth mak -

- ed.
- in'.

I hope you still _____ feel small _ when you
Don't let _____ some hell - bent _____

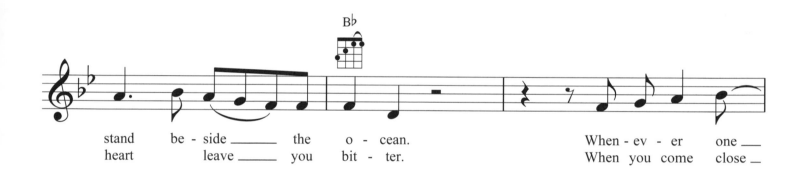

stand be - side _____ the o - cean.
heart leave _____ you bit - ter.

When - ev - er one _____
When you come close _

_____ door clos - es, I _____ hope one _ more o - pens.
_____ to sell - in' out, _____ re - con - sid - er.

Prom - ise me _____ that you'll _ give faith _____ a fight - ing
Give the heav - ens a - bove more _____ than just a pass - ing

chance. }
glance. }

And when you get the choice to

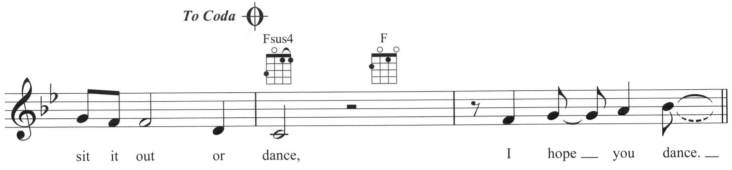

To Coda ⊕

sit it out or dance,

I hope — you dance. —

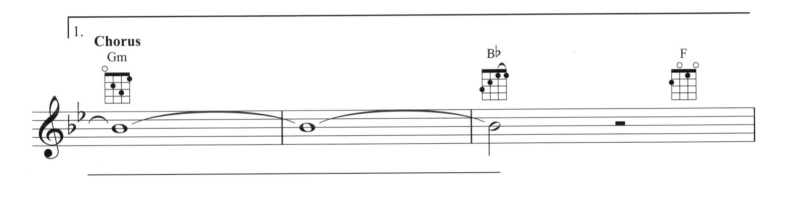

1.
Chorus

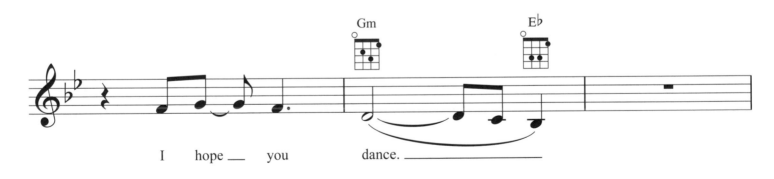

I hope — you dance. —

2.
Bridge-Chorus

2. I hope — you

(Time is a

50

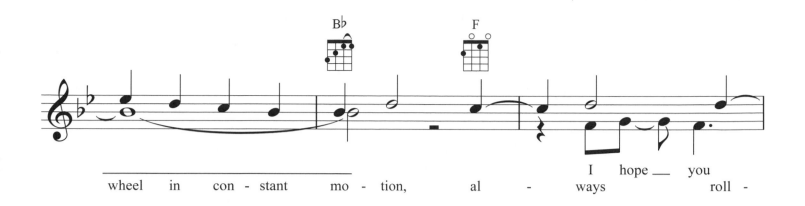

wheel in con - stant mo - tion, al - ways roll - I hope __ you

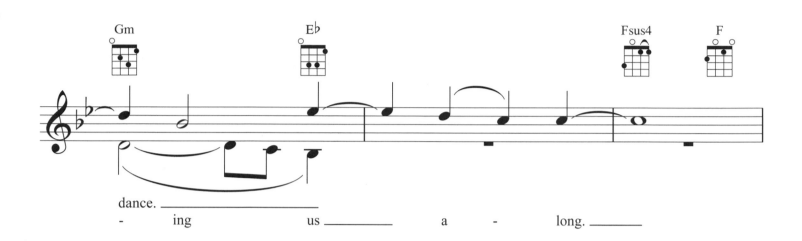

dance. __ - ing __ us __ a - long. __

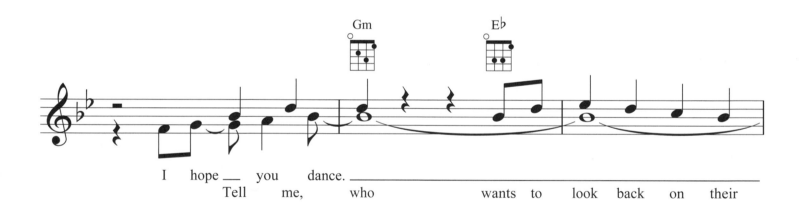

I hope __ you dance. __
Tell me, who wants to look back on their

youth and won - der where __ those years __
I hope __ you dance. __

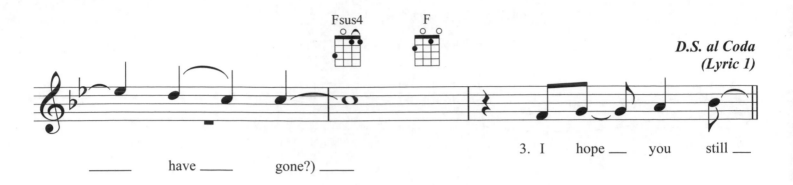

D.S. al Coda
(Lyric 1)

have _____ gone?) _____   3. I hope ___ you still ___

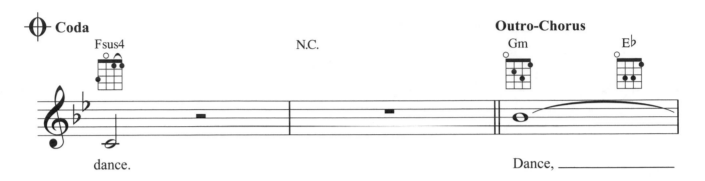

Coda   **Outro-Chorus**

dance.   Dance, _____

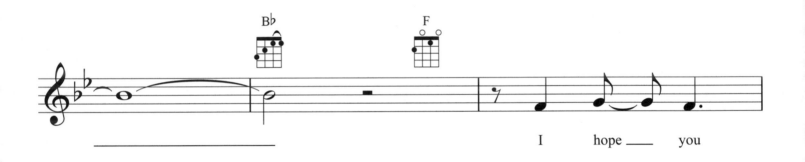

_____   I hope ___ you

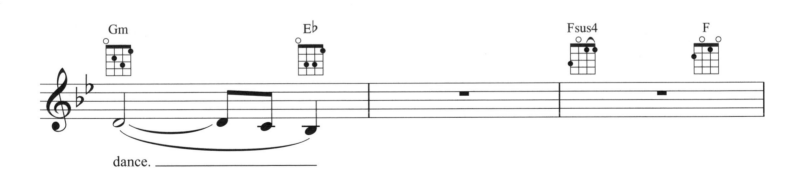

dance. _____

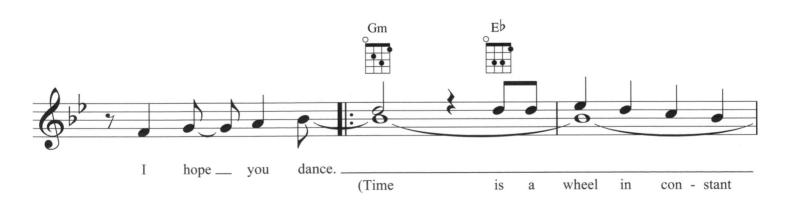

I hope ___ you dance. _____

(Time   is a   wheel   in con - stant

mo - tion,   al - ways   roll - ing   us ____

____ a - long. ____

who   wants to   look   back   on   their   youth   and   won -

- der   where ____ those   years ____ have ____ gone?) ____

____   I hope ____ you   dance. ____

Making Memories of Us

Words and Music by Rodney Crowell

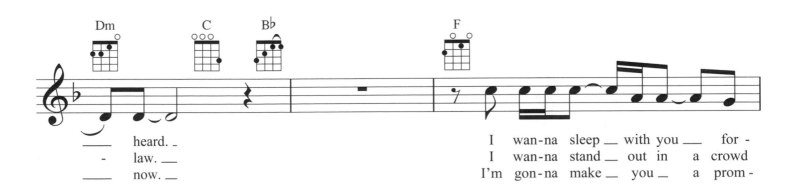

Copyright © 2004 Sony/ATV Music Publishing LLC, BMG Gold Songs and We Jam Writers Group
All Rights on behalf of Sony/ATV Music Publishing LLC Administered by Sony/ATV Music Publishing LLC,
424 Church Street, Suite 1200, Nashville, TN 37219
All Rights on behalf of BMG Gold Songs and We Jam Writers Group Administered by BMG Rights Management (US) LLC
International Copyright Secured   All Rights Reserved

ev - er _____ and I wan - na die _____ in your arms _____
for you, _____ a man a - mong men. _____
- ise, _____ if there's _ life _____ af - ter this, _____

_____
_____
_____

in a cab - in by a mead -
I wan - na make your world _ bet -
I'm gon - na be there _____ to meet

ow where the wild _ bees _____ swarm. _____
ter than it's ev - er _____ been. _____
you with a warm _ wet _____ kiss. _____

Chorus

And I'm gon - na love _____ you _____

like no - bod - y loves you. _____ And I'll earn _ your

To Coda

trust mak - ing mem'ries of _____ us. _____

1.

2.

55

Honey Bee

Words and Music by Rhett Akins and Ben Hayslip

© 2011 EMI BLACKWOOD MUSIC INC., RHETTNECK MUSIC, WB MUSIC CORP.,
MELISSA'S MONEY MUSIC PUBLISHING and GET A LOAD OF THIS MUSIC
All Rights for RHETTNECK MUSIC Controlled and Administered by EMI BLACKWOOD MUSIC INC.
All Rights for MELISSA'S MONEY MUSIC PUBLISHING and GET A LOAD OF THIS MUSIC Controlled and Administered by WB MUSIC CORP.
All Rights Reserved   International Copyright Secured   Used by Permission

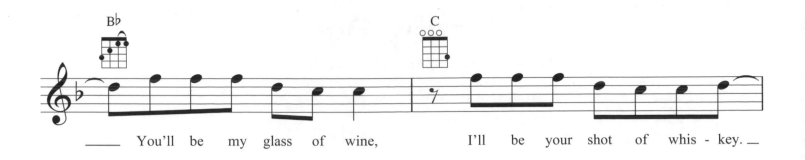

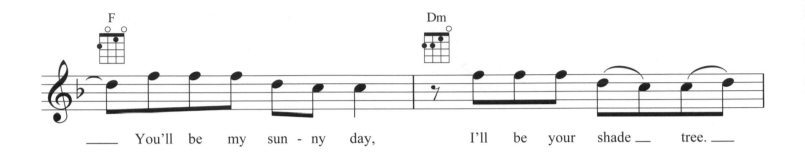

You'll be my glass of wine, I'll be your shot of whis-key.

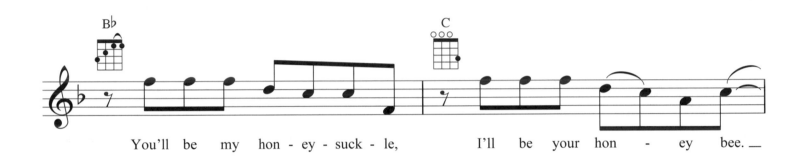

You'll be my sun-ny day, I'll be your shade __ tree. __

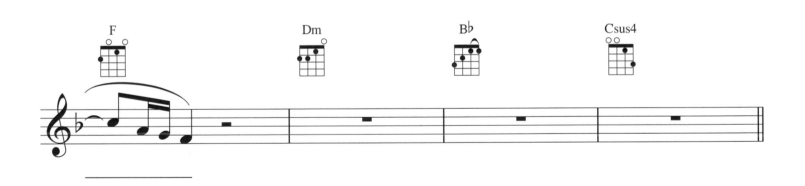

You'll be my hon-ey-suck-le, I'll be your hon - ey bee. __

𝄋 **Verse**

2. Yeah, that came out a lit-tle coun-try, but ev-'ry word was right __ on the mon-ey.
3. Your kiss just said it all. I'm __ glad we had __ this __ talk.

And I got you smil - in', hon - ey, right back at me. ___
Noth - in' left to do but fall in each oth - er's arms. ___

Now hold on 'cause I ____ ain't done. _ There's more where that ___ came from.
I could - a said, "I ____ love you," _ could - a wrote you a line or two.

Well, you know I'm just hav - in' fun, __ but se - ri - ous - ly. ___
Ba - by, all ____ I know to do ___ is speak right from the heart. ___

Chorus

You'll be my Loui - si - an - a, I'll be your Mis - sis - sip - pi. ___
You'll be my soft and sweet, I'll be your strong and stead - y. ___

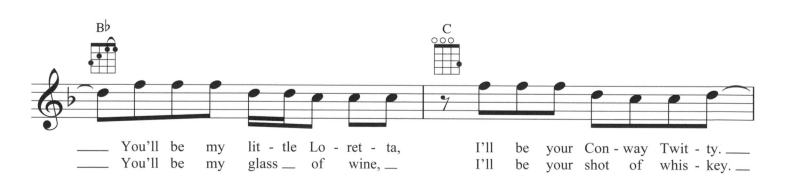

___ You'll be my lit - tle Lo - ret - ta, I'll be your Con - way Twit - ty. ___
___ You'll be my glass __ of wine, __ I'll be your shot of whis - key. ___

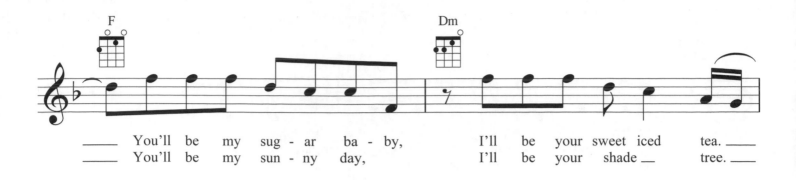

You'll be my sug - ar ba - by, I'll be your sweet iced tea.

You'll be my sun - ny day, I'll be your shade tree.

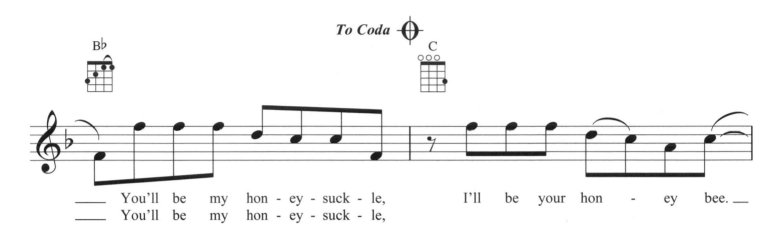

To Coda

You'll be my hon - ey - suck - le, I'll be your hon - ey bee.

You'll be my hon - ey - suck - le,

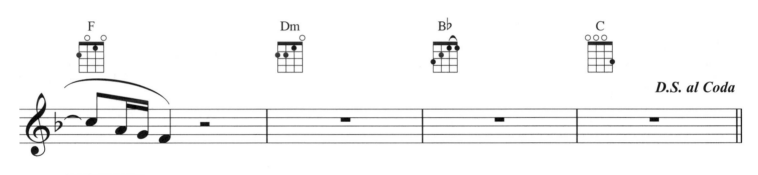

D.S. al Coda

Coda

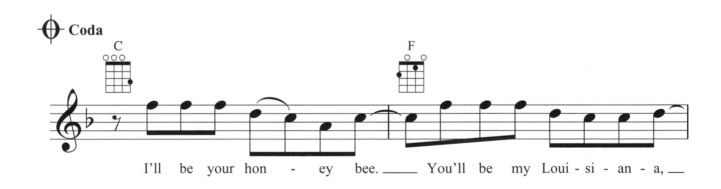

I'll be your hon - ey bee. You'll be my Loui - si - an - a,

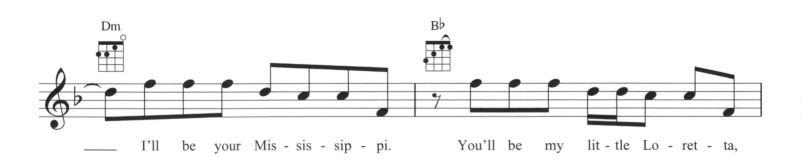

I'll be your Mis - sis - sip - pi. You'll be my lit - tle Lo - ret - ta,

I'll be your Con - way Twit - ty. _____ You'll be my sug - ar ba - by,

I'll be your sweet iced tea. _____ You'll be my hon - ey - suck - le

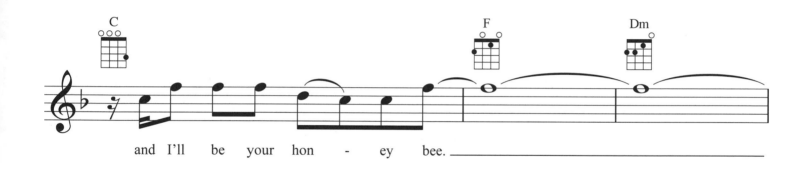

and I'll be your hon - ey bee. _____

_____ I'll be your hon - ey bee. _____

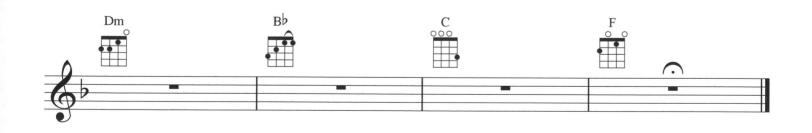

Need You Now

Words and Music by Hillary Scott, Charles Kelley, Dave Haywood and Josh Kear

© 2009 EMI FORAY MUSIC, HILLARY DAWN SONGS, WARNER-TAMERLANE PUBLISHING CORP.,
RADIOBULLETSPUBLISHING, DWHAYWOOD MUSIC, YEAR OF THE DOG MUSIC and DARTH BUDDHA
All Rights for HILLARY DAWN SONGS Controlled and Administered by EMI FORAY MUSIC
All Rights for RADIOBULLETSPUBLISHING and DWHAYWOOD MUSIC Administered by WARNER-TAMERLANE PUBLISHING CORP.
All Rights Reserved   International Copyright Secured   Used by Permission

It's a Great Day to Be Alive

Words and Music by Darrell Scott

© 1994, 1997 EMI APRIL MUSIC INC. and HOUSE OF BRAM
All Rights Controlled and Administered by EMI APRIL MUSIC INC.
All Rights Reserved   International Copyright Secured   Used by Permission

left it a - lone. _____ I hope they're do-in' al - right. 3. Now, I
- less as can be. _____ Lord, I guess he's do-in' al -

Chorus

right. And it's a great day to be a - live. ___ I know the

sun's still shin - in' when I close my eyes. There's some hard times in the

neigh - bor - hood, ___ but why ___ can't ev - 'ry day be just this good? _____

Bridge

_____ Some-times it's lone - ly, some-times it's on -

- ly me and the shad - ows that fill _____ this room.

Some - times I'm fall - in',

des - p'rate-ly ____ call - in', howl - in' at ____ the moon. __

Interlude

Ow - ooh. ____

Ow - ooh. ____

Verse

4. Well, __ I might go get me a new _

__ tat - too or take my old Har - ley for a three - day cruise.

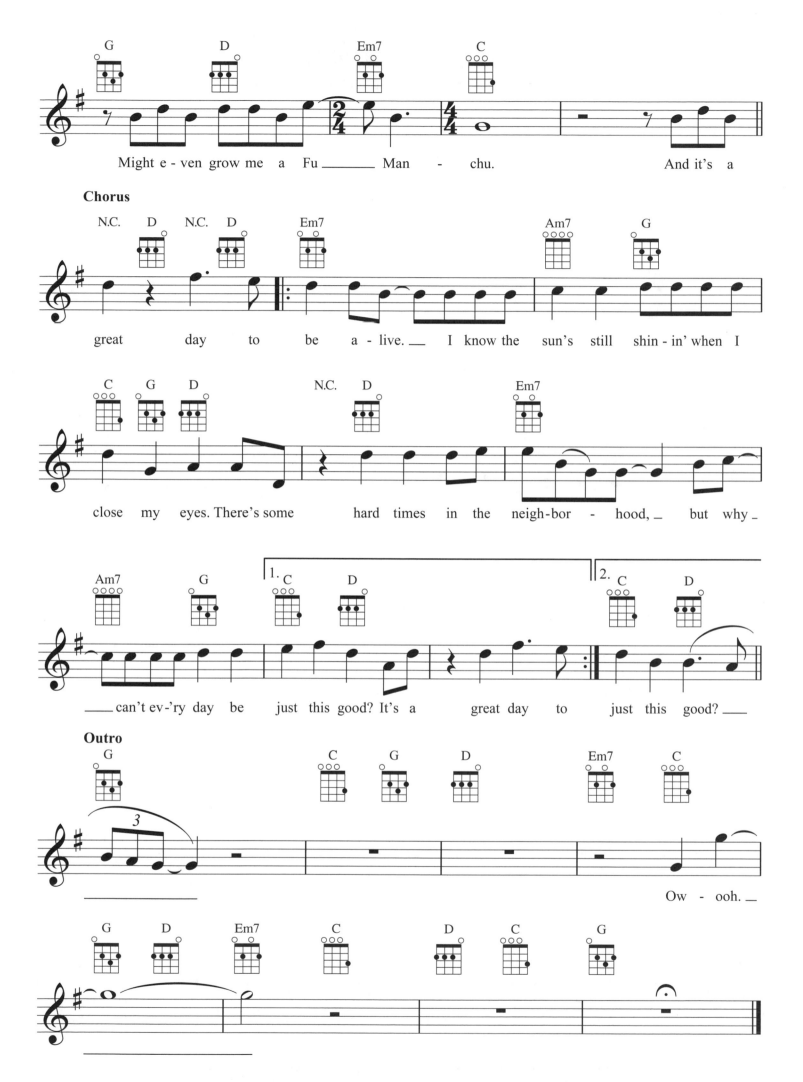

Might e - ven grow me a Fu _____ Man - chu.   And it's a

Chorus

great   day   to   be   a - live. __ I know the   sun's still   shin - in' when I

close   my   eyes. There's some   hard   times   in the   neigh-bor - hood, __ but why __

__ can't ev-'ry day   be   just this good? It's a   great day   to   just this   good? __

Outro

_____

Ow - ooh. __

_____

Remind Me

Words and Music by Kelley Lovelace, Brad Paisley and Chris DuBois

© 2011 EMI APRIL MUSIC INC., DIDN'T HAVE TO BE MUSIC and HOUSE OF SEA GAYLE MUSIC
All Rights for DIDN'T HAVE TO BE MUSIC Controlled and Administered by EMI APRIL MUSIC INC.
All Rights Reserved   International Copyright Secured   Used by Permission

Chorus

feel that way a - gain. _____ Been so long ___ that

you ___ for - get ___ the way _____ I used ___ to kiss ___

___ your neck. ___ *Female:* Re - mind ___ me. ___ Re - mind _

_____ me. _____ *Male:* So _____ on fire _____ and so _

___ in love ___ way ___ back when ___ we could - n't

get e - nough. *Female:* Re - mind ___ me, _____ re - mind _

Chorus

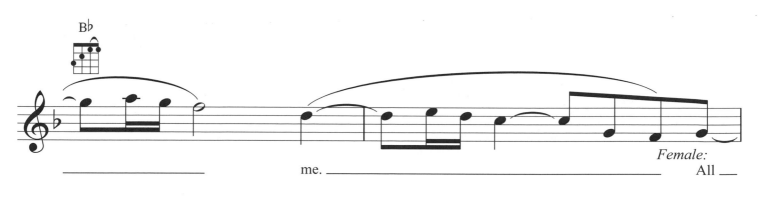

Female: me. All

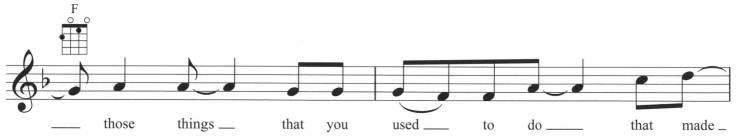

those things that you used to do that made

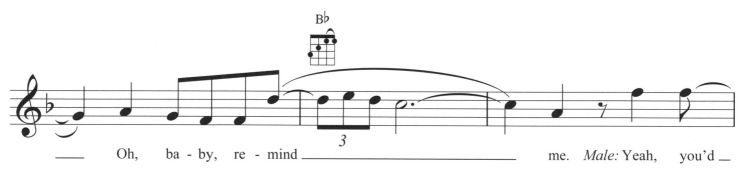

me fall in love with you. Re-mind me.

Oh, ba-by, re - mind me. _Male:_ Yeah, you'd

wake up in my old T - shirt, all

those morn-ings I was late for work. Re - mind me.

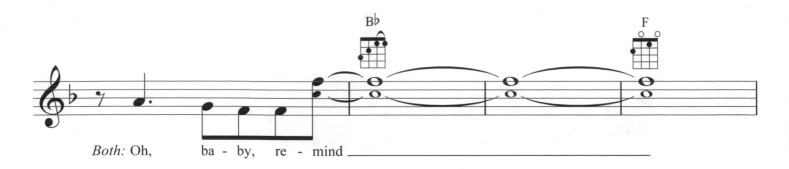

Both: Oh, ba - by, re - mind _____

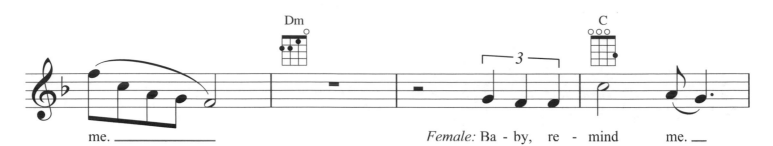

me. _____ Female: Ba - by, re - mind me. _____

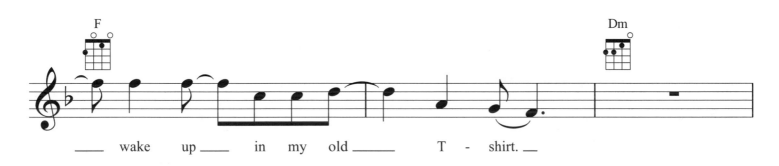

Ba - by, re - mind _____ me. Male: Yeah, you'd _____

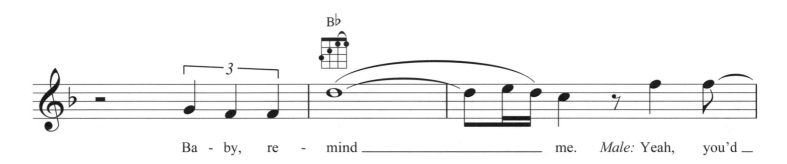

_____ wake up _____ in my old _____ T - shirt. _____

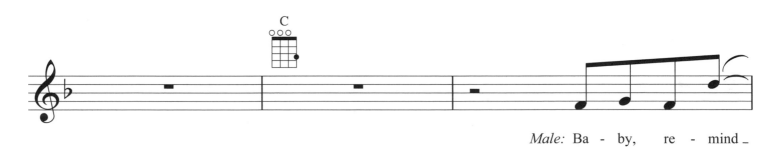

Male: Ba - by, re - mind _____

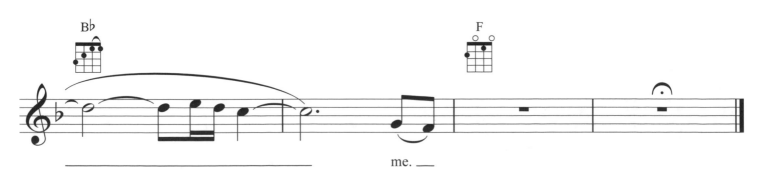

_____ me. _____

Springsteen

Words and Music by Eric Church, Jeffery Hyde and Ryan Tyndell

1. To this day ___ when I hear that song, ___ I see you stand - in' there on that lawn, ___ dis-count shades, ___ store-bought tan, ___ flip - flops and cut-off jeans. ___

Some-where be-tween that set-tin' sun, ___ I'm on fire ___ and born to run. ___ You looked at me ___ and I was done. ___ We're just get-tin' start - ed. I was

sing-in' to you, ___ you were sing-in' to me. ___ I was so a - live, ___ nev - er been more free. ___ Fired

Copyright © 2011 Sony/ATV Music Publishing LLC, Sinnerlina Music, BMG Bumblebee, Mammaw's Cornbread Music and Purple Cape Music/ole
All Rights on behalf of Sony/ATV Music Publishing LLC and Sinnerlina Music Administered by
Sony/ATV Music Publishing LLC, 424 Church Street, Suite 1200, Nashville, TN 37219
All Rights on behalf of BMG Bumblebee and Mammaw's Cornbread Music Administered by BMG Rights Management (US) LLC
International Copyright Secured   All Rights Reserved

up my dad-dy's light - er and we ___ sang, "Oh." _____

Stayed there ___ till they forced us out ___ and took the long ___ way to your house. ___

I can still ___ hear the sound ___ of you say - in', "Don't go." _____

𝄋 Chorus

When I think a - bout you, I think a - bout sev - en - teen. ___
When you think a - bout me, do you think a - bout sev - en - teen? ___

I think a - bout my old Jeep, I think a - bout the stars in the sky. ⎫
Do you think a - bout my old Jeep, think a - bout the stars in the sky? ⎭

Fun - ny how a mel - o - dy _____ sounds like a mem - o - ry, _____

like ___ a sound - track ___ to a Ju - ly Sat - ur - day ___ night, _

To Coda ⊕

___ Spring - steen.

Verse

2. I bumped in - to you ___ by hap-pen - stance. _ You

prob-'ly would-n't e-ven know who I am. ___ But if I whis-pered your name, I bet ___ there'd

still be a spark ___ from back when I _____ was gas - o - line ___ and this old _

___ tat - too ___ had brand - new ink ___ and we did-n't care what your ma-ma'd think _'bout your

name on my arm. _____ Ba - by, is it spring or is it sum - mer, the

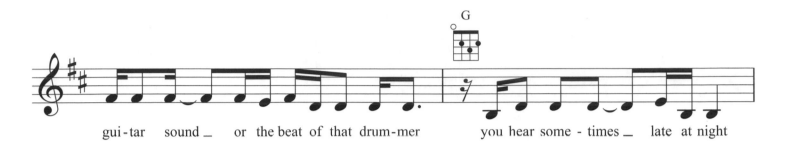

gui - tar sound _ or the beat of that drum - mer you hear some - times _ late at night

on your ra - di - o? ____ E - ven though you're a mil - lion miles _ a - way, _ when

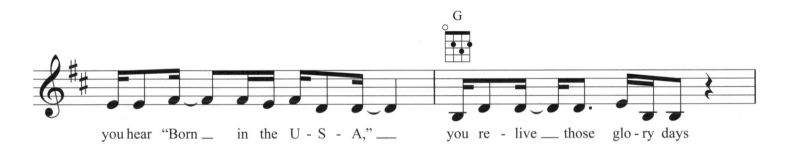

you hear "Born _ in the U - S - A," _ you re - live _ those glo - ry days

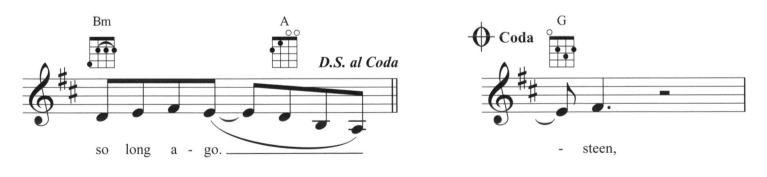

so long a - go. _____   - steen,

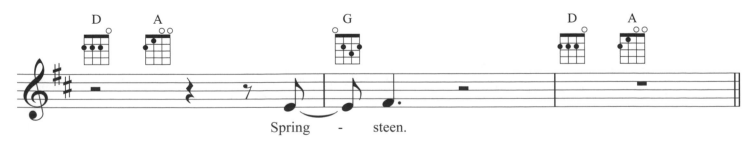

Spring - steen.

Bridge

Whoa whoa whoa — oh, whoa whoa whoa — oh, whoa whoa whoa — oh,

1.
whoa whoa. _____

2. **Outro-Chorus**
whoa whoa. _____ Fun-ny how a mel-o-dy ___

sounds like a mem-o-ry, ___ like ___ a sound - track to a

Ju - ly Sat-ur-day ___ night, ___ Spring - steen,

Spring - steen.

Three Wooden Crosses

Words and Music by Kim Williams and Doug Johnson

1. A farm - er and ___ a teach - er, a
(2.) farm - er left ___ a har - vest, a

hook - er and a preach - er, rid - in' on ___ a mid -
home and eight - y a - cres, the faith and love ___ for grow -

- night bus, ___ bound for Mex - i - co. ___ One was
- in' things _ bound in his young son's _ heart. And that

head - ed for ___ va - ca - tion, one for
teach - er left ___ her wis - dom in the

high - er ed - u - ca - tion and two of them ___ were search -
minds ___ of lots of chil - dren. Did her best to give ___ 'em all ___

Copyright © 2002 Sony/ATV Music Publishing LLC, Mike Curb Music and Sweet Radical Music
All Rights on behalf of Sony/ATV Music Publishing LLC Administered by Sony/ATV Music Publishing LLC,
424 Church Street, Suite 1200, Nashville, TN 37219
All Rights on behalf of Sweet Radical Music Administered by Mike Curb Music
International Copyright Secured   All Rights Reserved

-in' for _____ lost souls. That

_____ a bet - ter start. And that

Pre-Chorus

driv - er nev - er ev - er saw _____ the stop _____ sign,
preach - er whis - pered, "Can't _____ you see _____ the prom - ised land?"

and eight - een - wheel - ers can't _____ stop on a dime. _____
as he lay his blood-stained Bi - ble in _____ that hook-er's hand. _____

Chorus

There are three wood - en cross-

- es on _____ the right _____ side of _____ the high - way.

Why there's not four of them, _ (1., 2.) heav - en on - ly knows. _____
(D.S.) now I guess _____ we know. _____

83

he said, "Bless the farm - er and the

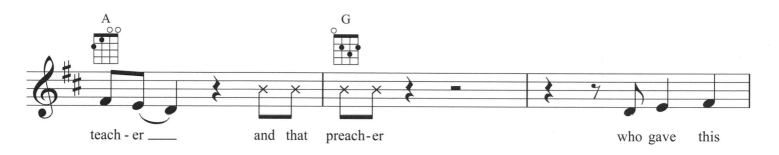

teach - er and that preach-er who gave this

Bi - ble to my ma - ma who read it to me."

D.S. al Coda

There are

Outro

Coda

There are three wood - en cross -

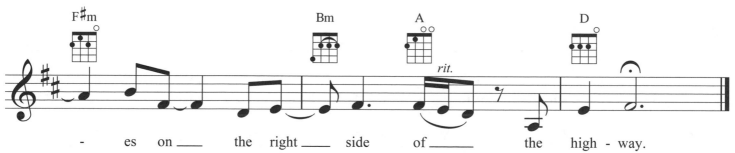

- es on the right side of the high - way.

85

What About Now

Words and Music by Ron Harbin, Anthony Smith and Aaron Barker

Copyright © 2000 Sony/ATV Music Publishing LLC, Ron Harbin Music, O-Tex Music, Blind Sparrow Music, WB Music Corp. and Notes to Music
All Rights on behalf of Sony/ATV Music Publishing LLC and Ron Harbin Music Administered by Sony/ATV Music Publishing LLC,
424 Church Street, Suite 1200, Nashville, TN 37219
All Rights on behalf of Blind Sparrow Music Administered by O-Tex Music
International Copyright Secured   All Rights Reserved

_____ where it goes, ___ but it beats ___ where we're at. _____ We al -
_____ me the word ___ and we'll be kick - in' up dust. ___ We _

- ways said ___ some - day _____ some - how ___ we're gon - na
_____ both know ___ it's just a mat - ter of time ___ till our _____

get a - way, ___ gon - na blow _____ this town. ___
hearts start rac - in' for that coun - ty line. ___

%̸ Chorus

What a - bout ___ now? _____ How 'bout to - night? _

Ba - by, for once _____ let's don't ___ think ___ twice. __

Let's take _____ that spin ___ that nev - er ends ___ that _ we've _

been talk - in' a - bout. _____ What a - bout _____ now? _

Why should we wait? _____ We can chase _____ these dreams _ down the in-

ter - state _____ and be _____ long gone _____ 'fore the world _

_____ moves on _____ and _____ makes _____ an - oth - er round. _

1.

_____ What a - bout _____ now? _____

2. We've been put - _____ What a - bout _____ now? _____

What Hurts the Most

Words and Music by Steve Robson and Jeffrey Steele

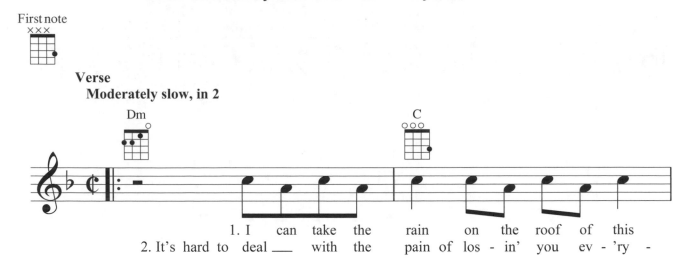

Verse
Moderately slow, in 2

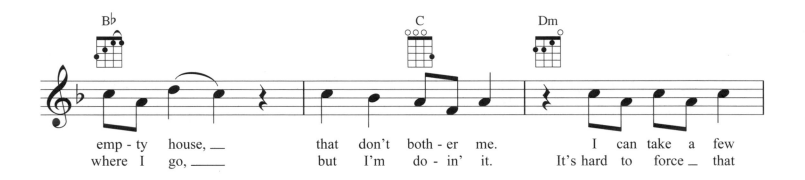

1. I can take the rain on the roof of this
2. It's hard to deal __ with the pain of los - in' you ev - 'ry -

emp - ty house, __ that don't both - er me. I can take a few
where I go, __ but I'm do - in' it. It's hard to force __ that

tears now and then and just let 'em out. ____ I'm not a -
smile when I see our old friends and I'm a - lone. Still hard - er

fraid to cry, ev - 'ry once in a while e - ven though
get - tin' up, get - tin' dressed, liv - in' with this re - gret.

Copyright © 2005 RONDOR MUSIC (LONDON) LTD., SONGS OF WINDSWEPT PACIFIC and GOTTAHAVEABLE MUSIC
All Rights for RONDOR MUSIC (LONDON) LTD. in the U.S. and Canada Controlled and Administered by ALMO MUSIC CORP.
All Rights for SONGS OF WINDSWEPT PACIFIC Administered by BMG RIGHTS MANAGEMENT (US) LLC
All Rights for GOTTAHAVEABLE MUSIC Administered by BPJ ADMINISTRATION, P.O. BOX 218061, Nashville, TN 37221
All Rights Reserved   Used by Permission

Stuck Like Glue

Words and Music by Kristian Bush, Shy Carter, Kevin Griffin and Jennifer Nettles

Copyright © 2010 BMG Platinum Songs, Control Group Music, BMG Rights Management (UK) Ltd.,
Worldwide EMG Music B, You Want How Much Of What Publishing and Jennifer Nettles Publishing
All Rights for BMG Platinum Songs, Control Group Music, BMG Rights Management (UK) Ltd., Worldwide EMG Music B
and You Want How Much Of What Publishing Administered by BMG Rights Management (US) LLC
All Rights Reserved   Used by Permission

And just when I, _____ I start to think _ they're right, _

%. Chorus

_ that love has died, _ there _ you go mak-in' my heart _

_ beat a-gain, heart _ beat a-gain, heart _ beat a-gain. _ There _

_ you go mak-in' me feel _ like a kid. Won't you do it, do it one

time? There _ you go pull-in' me right _ back in, _ right _

_ back in, _ right _ back in, and I know _____

When it does - n't mat - ter who's right, fight a - bout it all night,

had e - nough, __ you give me that look. I'm sor -

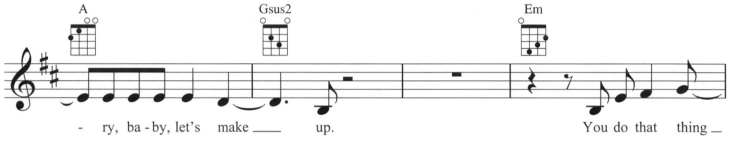

- ry, ba - by, let's make ____ up. You do that thing __

D.S. al Coda

____ that makes __ me laugh. ____ And just like that, ____ there __

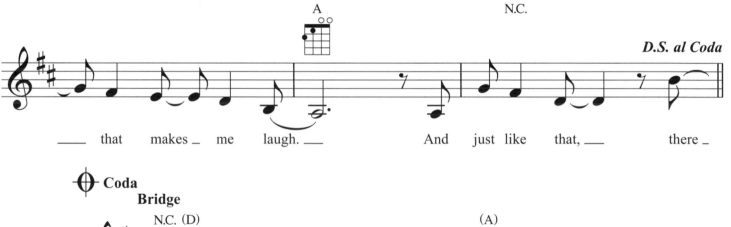

⊕ Coda
Bridge

N.C. (D) (A)

Wuh oh, ____ wuh oh, you al - most stay out,

(Gsus2) (D)

too stuck to - geth - er from the A - T - L. ____ Wuh oh, ____ wuh oh,

Wuh, oh, ___ wuh oh,   wuh oh, ___ wuh oh,   stuck like glue.

You and me to - geth - er, say it's all I wan - na do. I said there ___

Chorus

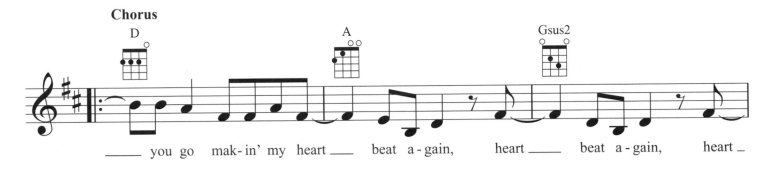

___ you go mak - in' my heart ___ beat a - gain, heart ___ beat a - gain, heart ___

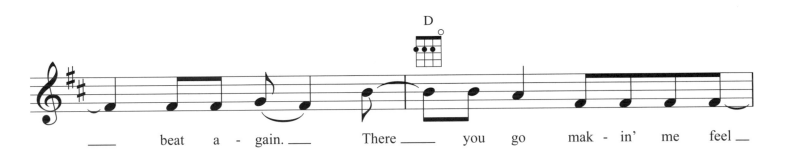

___ beat a - gain. ___ There ___ you go mak - in' me feel ___

___ like a kid. Won't you do it, do it one

time?   There ___ you go pull - in' me right ___ back in, ___ right ___

Where Were You
(When the World Stopped Turning)

Words and Music by Alan Jackson

© 2001 EMI APRIL MUSIC INC. and TRI-ANGELS MUSIC
All Rights Controlled and Administered by EMI APRIL MUSIC INC.
All Rights Reserved   International Copyright Secured   Used by Permission

Red, White and Blue ___ and he - roes who died just
think of to - mor - row, go out and buy you a

do - in' what ___ they do? Did you look up to heav - en for
gun? Did you turn off that vio - lent old

some kind ___ of an - swer and look at your - self ___ and
mov - ie ___ you're watch - in' and

Chorus

what real - ly mat - ters? I'm just a sing - er of ___

sim - ple songs. ___ I'm not a real po - lit - i - cal ___ man. I watch

C - N - N, ___ but I'm not ___ sure I can tell you the

dif-f'rence in I - raq and I - ran. But I know Je - sus and I ___

___ talk to God ___ and I re - mem - ber this from when I was

young: Faith, hope and love are some good things He gave us,

D.C. al Coda

and the great - est is love.

Coda

turn on "I Love Lu - cy" re - runs? Did you

go to a church ___ and hold hands with some stran - ger,

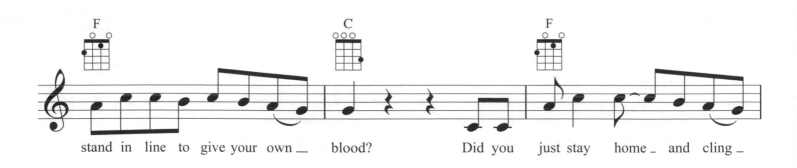

stand in line to give your own __ blood? Did you just stay home __ and cling __

tight __ to your fam -'ly, thank God you have some - bod - y to love? ___

Chorus

I'm just a sing - er of ___ sim - ple songs. __ I'm not a

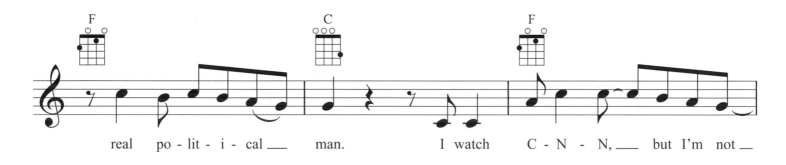

real po - lit - i - cal ___ man. I watch C - N - N, ___ but I'm not ___

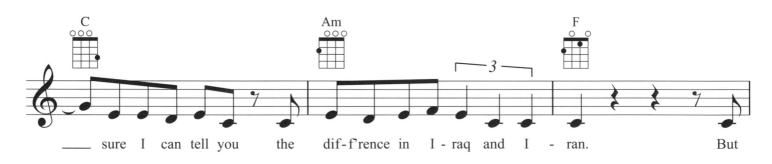

___ sure I can tell you the dif - f'rence in I - raq and I - ran. But

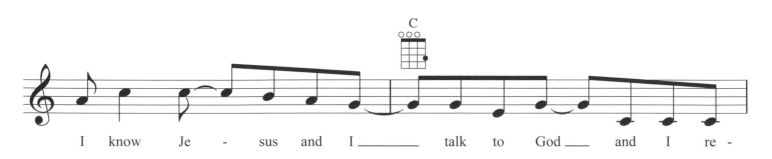

I know Je - sus and I _____ talk to God ___ and I re -

mem-ber this from when I was young: Faith, hope and love are some

good things   He gave us,   and the great-est   is   love.

love,   and the great-est   is   love,

and the great-est   is   love.

Outro

Where were   you   when the   world ____ stopped turn-in'

that   Sep-tem-ber   day? ____

You Belong with Me

Words and Music by Taylor Swift and Liz Rose

Copyright © 2008 Sony/ATV Music Publishing LLC, Taylor Swift Music, Potting Shed Music and Barbara Orbison World Publishing
All Rights on behalf of Sony/ATV Music Publishing LLC and Taylor Swift Music Administered by
Sony/ATV Music Publishing LLC, 424 Church Street, Suite 1200, Nashville, TN 37219
All Rights on behalf of Potting Shed Music and Barbara Orbison World Publishing Administered by BMG Rights Management (US) LLC
International Copyright Secured   All Rights Reserved

mu - sic she does - n't like, _____ and she'll nev - er
while since she brought you down. _____ You say you're fine; I know you

know your sto - ry like I do.
bet - ter than that. Hey, what - cha do - ing with a

Pre-Chorus

girl like that?
She wears wears short high skirts, heels,

But she wears short skirts,

I wear T - shirts, } she's cheer cap - tain and I'm on the bleach - ers,
I wear sneak - ers, }

dream - ing 'bout the day when you'll wake up and find _____ that what you're

look - ing for _____ has been here _____ the whole time. If you could

§ **Chorus**

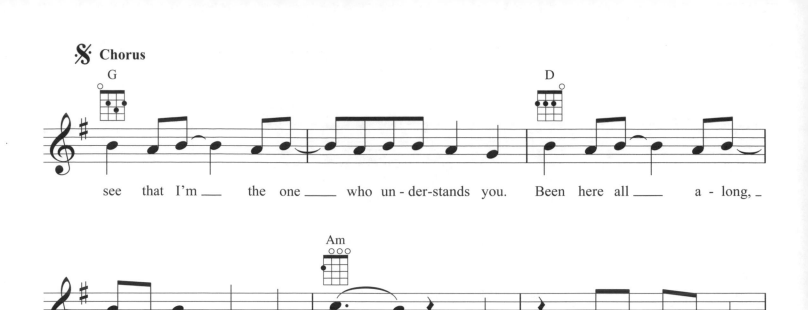

see that I'm ___ the one ___ who un-der-stands you. Been here all ___ a-long, ___

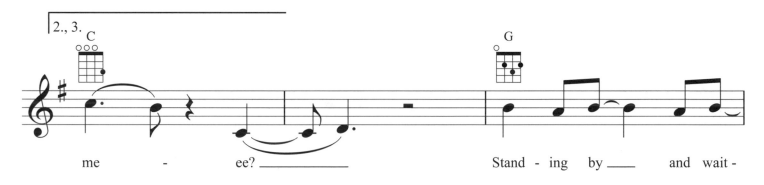

___ so why can't you see - ee you be-long ___ with

1.

me - ee? ___ You be-long ___ with me. ___

2., 3.

me - ee? ___ Stand-ing by ___ and wait-

- ing at your back door. All this time, ___ how could ___ you not know, ___ ba-

by - y, you be-long ___ with me - ee? ___

To Coda ⊕ G

_____ You be - long _ with me. _____

Bridge
Am

Oh, I re - mem - ber you driv - ing to my house in the

C   G

mid - dle of the night. I'm the one who makes you laugh when you

D   Am

know you're 'bout to cry. I know your fa - v'rite songs, and you

C   G

tell me 'bout your dreams. Think I know where you be - long. Think I

D   **D.S. al Coda**
                     (take 2nd ending)   ⊕ **Coda** G

know it's with me. _____   Can't you

Your Man

Words and Music by Jace Everett, Chris DuBois and Chris Stapleton

Ba - by, lock the door and turn the lights down low ___

and put some mu - sic on that's soft and slow. ___ Ba - by, we ain't got no

place ___ to go. ___ I hope you un - der - stand I've been think - in' 'bout this

all day long. ___ Nev - er felt a feel - in' quite ___ this strong. ___

I can't be - lieve how much it turns ___ me on ___ just to be your man.

Copyright © 2004, 2005, 2006 EMI Blackwood Music Inc., New Sea Gayle Music and WB Music Corp.
All Rights on behalf of EMI Blackwood Music Inc. Administered by Sony/ATV Music Publishing LLC,
424 Church Street, Suite 1200, Nashville, TN 37219
International Copyright Secured   All Rights Reserved

HAL·LEONARD UKULELE PLAY-ALONG

Now you can play your favorite songs on your uke with great-sounding backing tracks to help you sound like a bona fide pro! This series includes the Amazing Slow Downer, so you can adjust the tempo without changing the pitch.

1. POP HITS
00701451 Book/CD Pack........................$14.99

2. UKE CLASSICS
00701452 Book/CD Pack........................$12.99

3. HAWAIIAN FAVORITES
00701453 Book/CD Pack........................$12.99

4. CHILDREN'S SONGS
00701454 Book/CD Pack........................$12.99

5. CHRISTMAS SONGS
00701696 Book/CD Pack........................$12.99

6. LENNON & MCCARTNEY
00701723 Book/CD Pack........................$12.99

7. DISNEY FAVORITES
00701724 Book/CD Pack........................$12.99

8. CHART HITS
00701745 Book/CD Pack........................$14.99

9. THE SOUND OF MUSIC
00701784 Book/CD Pack........................$12.99

10. MOTOWN
00701964 Book/CD Pack........................$12.99

11. CHRISTMAS STRUMMING
00702458 Book/CD Pack........................$12.99

12. BLUEGRASS FAVORITES
00702584 Book/CD Pack........................$12.99

13. UKULELE SONGS
00702599 Book/CD Pack........................$12.99

14. JOHNNY CASH
00702615 Book/CD Pack........................$14.99

15. COUNTRY CLASSICS
00702834 Book/CD Pack........................$12.99

16. STANDARDS
00702835 Book/CD Pack........................$12.99

17. POP STANDARDS
00702836 Book/CD Pack........................$12.99

18. IRISH SONGS
00703086 Book/CD Pack........................$12.99

19. BLUES STANDARDS
00703087 Book/CD Pack........................$12.99

20. FOLK POP ROCK
00703088 Book/CD Pack........................$12.99

21. HAWAIIAN CLASSICS
00703097 Book/CD Pack........................$12.99

22. ISLAND SONGS
00703098 Book/CD Pack........................$12.99

23. TAYLOR SWIFT
00704106 Book/CD Pack........................$14.99

24. WINTER WONDERLAND
00101871 Book/CD Pack........................$12.99

25. GREEN DAY
00110398 Book/CD Pack........................$14.99

26. BOB MARLEY
00110399 Book/CD Pack........................$14.99

27. TIN PAN ALLEY
00116358 Book/CD Pack........................$12.99

28. STEVIE WONDER
00116736 Book/CD Pack........................$14.99

30. ACOUSTIC SONGS
00122336 Book/CD Pack........................$14.99

32. TOP DOWNLOADS
00127507 Book/CD Pack........................$14.99

34. CHRISTMAS HITS
00128602 Book/CD Pack........................$14.99

HAL·LEONARD® CORPORATION

7777 W. BLUEMOUND RD. P.O. BOX 13819 MILWAUKEE, WI 53213

www.halleonard.com

Prices, contents, and availability subject to change without notice.

0814